Your Senses

by Helen Frost

Consulting Editor: Gail Saunders-Smith, Ph.D.

Consultant: Eric H. Chudler, Ph.D.
Research Associate Professor
Department of Anesthesiology
University of Washington, Seattle

Pebble Books

an imprint of Capstone Press
Mankato, Minnesota

Pebble Books are published by Capstone Press
1710 Roe Crest Drive, North Mankato, Minnesota 56003
http://www.capstone-press.com

062012
006741R

Library of Congress Cataloging-in-Publication Data
Frost, Helen, 1949–
     Your senses / by Helen Frost.
     p. cm.—(The senses)
     Includes bibliographical references and index.
     Summary: Simple text and photographs present the five senses and how they
work together.
     ISBN-13: 978-0-7368-0387-8 (hardcover)
     ISBN-10: 0-7368-0387-4 (hardcover)
     ISBN-13. 978-0-7368-4869-5 (paperback)
     ISBN-10: 0-7368-4869-X (paperback)
     1. Senses and sensation—Juvenile literature. [1. Senses and sensation.] I. Title.
II. Series: Frost, Helen, 1949– The senses.
QP434.F76 2000
612.8— dc21   98-18966
                                                                              CIP

Note to Parents and Teachers

The Senses series supports national science standards for units related to behavioral science. This book describes and illustrates the five senses. The photographs support early readers in understanding the text. The repetition of words and phrases helps early readers learn new words. This book also introduces early readers to subject-specific vocabulary words, which are defined in the Words to Know section. Early readers may need assistance to read some words and to use the Table of Contents, Words to Know, Read More, Internet Sites, and Index/Word List sections of the book.

Table of Contents

4

You have five senses.
Your senses let you
see, hear, smell,
taste, and touch.

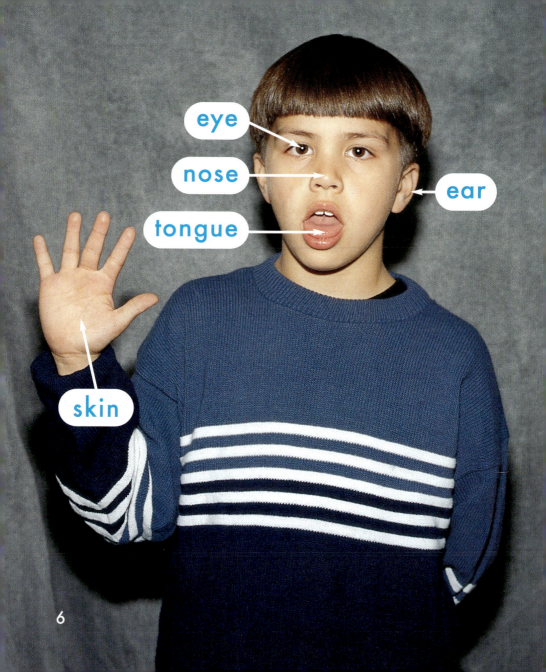

eye

nose

ear

tongue

skin

6

Your eyes, ears, nose, tongue, and skin have sensors. The sensors send signals to your brain.

Your brain understands the signals. The signals tell you about everything around you.

You see with your eyes. You see shapes, sizes, and colors.

You hear with your ears. You hear high sounds and low sounds. You hear soft sounds and loud sounds.

You smell with your nose. You like some smells. You do not like other smells.

You taste with your tongue. You taste sweet foods and sour foods. You taste bitter foods and salty foods.

You touch with your skin. You touch hot things and cold things. You touch soft things and hard things.

Your senses work together. They help you understand what is around you.

Words to Know

bitter—a strong and unsweet taste; orange peels taste bitter.

brain—the body part inside your head that controls your body; your brain understands the signals that your senses send.

nerve—a bundle of thin fibers that sends signals between your brain and other parts of your body

sense—a way of knowing about things around you; hearing, seeing, smelling, tasting, and touching are your five senses.

sensor—a cell that detects things around you; sensors send signals to your brain.

signal—a message; signals travel along nerves to your brain.

sour—a strong, acid taste; lemons taste sour.

Read More

Bennett, Paul. *My Brain and Senses*. Bodyworks. Parsippany, N.J.: Silver Press, 1998.

Maurer, Tracy. *The Senses. Bodyworks*. Vero Beach, Fla.: Rourke, 1999.

Parker, Steve. *Senses*. Look at Your Body. Brookfield, Conn.: Copper Beech Books, 1997.

Tatchell, Judy. *How Do Your Senses Work?* Flip Flaps. London: Usborne Publishing, 1997.

Internet Sites

FactHound offers a safe, fun way to find Internet sites related to this book. All of the sites on FactHound have been researched by our staff.

Here's all you do:

Visit *www.facthound.com*

FactHound will fetch the best sites for you!

23

Index/Word List

Word Count: 138
Early-Intervention Level: 14

Editorial Credits

Mari C. Schuh, editor; Timothy Halldin, cover designer; Kimberly Danger,
photo researcher

Photo Credits

Bill Losh/FPG International LLC, cover
David F. Clobes, 4 (bottom right), 6, 18
Index Stock Imagery, 4 (top right), 8
Photo Network/Tom McCarthy, 4 (top left); Myrleen Cate, 4 (bottom left), 10, 12
Unicorn Stock Photos/Martha McBride, 16
Uniphoto, 1, 20
Visuals Unlimited/Bill Beatty, 4 (center); Dick Thomas, 14